SPORTS HEROES AND LEGENDS

Barry Bonds

Read all of the books in this exciting,
action-packed biography series!

Hank Aaron

Muhammad Ali

Lance Armstrong

Barry Bonds

Roberto Clemente

Joe DiMaggio

Tim Duncan

Dale Earnhardt Jr.

Lou Gehrig

Mia Hamm

Tony Hawk

Derek Jeter

Michael Jordan

Sandy Koufax

Michelle Kwan

Mickey Mantle

Shaquille O'Neal

Jesse Owens

Jackie Robinson

Alex Rodriguez

Wilma Rudolf

Babe Ruth

Ichiro Suzuki

Tiger Woods

SPORTS HEROES AND LEGENDS

Barry Bonds

by Ross Bernstein

BARNES
& NOBLE

NEW YORK

For Campbell

This 2004 edition published by Barnes & Noble, Inc. by arrangement
with Lerner Publications Company, a division of Lerner Publishing Group,
Minneapolis, MN.

Cover photograph: © Mickey Pfleger/ENDZONE

Sports Heroes and Legends™ is a trademark of Barnes & Noble, Inc.

Barnes & Noble, Inc.
122 Fifth Avenue
New York, NY 10011

ISBN-13: 978-0-7607-5060-5
ISBN-10: 0-7607-5060-2

Printed and bound in the United States of America

10 9 8 7 6 5 4 3

Contents

Breaking the Record

It was late September 2001, and slowly but surely San Francisco Giants left fielder Barry Bonds was making history. He was just one home run away from tying St. Louis Cardinals slugger Mark McGwire's single-season record of seventy home runs, set three years earlier. The pressure on Barry was intense. The media swarmed relentlessly, and he struggled to keep himself together.

With just a few games left in the season, Barry's biggest battle was just getting a pitch to hit. Most pitchers didn't want to pitch to him. They preferred to throw him four balls for a walk rather than go down in history as the pitcher who gave up home run number seventy. As a result, Barry was being walked so often that he actually broke the great Babe Ruth's single-season walk record of 170. Time was running out.

Finally on October 4, Barry got his big break when Houston

Astros reliever Wilfredo Rodriguez hung a slider that Barry pounded more than 450 feet into the upper deck at Houston's Enron Field. He'd done it. He'd tied McGwire's record! The Houston crowd gave him a long standing ovation, and his teammates mobbed him at home plate after he rounded third.

After the game, Barry spoke with reporters, telling them that it hadn't been easy to hit number seventy. "When [Rodriguez] threw the first pitch, I just was, 'Wow!' It's really rare when you see left-handers that throw [that hard]," said Barry.

And if he hadn't been under enough strain during recent games, Barry felt even more pressure with just one more homer needed to break the record once and for all. The following day, Barry also had to battle grief as he attended the funeral for Franklin Bradley. Bradley had been Barry's close friend and bodyguard.

Barry tried to stay strong. He went to the ballpark that night to face the Los Angeles Dodgers, dedicating the game to his fallen friend. With that, Barry stepped up to bat in the first inning and promptly crushed a fastball from pitcher Chan Ho Park 442 feet into the right-field arcade to break the record. The crowd cheered even louder than the crowd had the night before. After Barry crossed home plate, he pointed up to the heavens in recognition of his friend. Then he picked up his eleven-year-old son, Nikolai, a San Francisco batboy, who had run to home plate to celebrate the moment with his father.

Believe it or not, Barry wasn't finished hitting homers. Just two innings later, he hit number seventy-two off of Park. This one was a 407-foot rocket to center field. Barry had just left Mark McGwire's record in the dust. And there was still one game left in the season!

In that final game, Barry put an exclamation point on his historic season by nailing his seventy-third and final home run of the year off of Dodgers knuckleballer Dennis Springer. It was a solo shot in the first inning at Pac Bell Park, the Giants' home field. Dozens of fans dove on top of one another to try to grab this rare piece of sports history.

"This was a great, great way to end it with a victory and a home run," Bonds said after the game. "You can't ask for anything better. I never thought I could do it." Although Barry's success may have taken him by surprise, other people had seen it coming. After all, it was a moment he'd been preparing for since the day he first picked up a bat.

Chapter One

In the Shadows of Greatness

Barry Lamar Bonds was born on July 24, 1964, in Riverside, California. The eldest of Bobby and Pat Bonds's four children—who also included Cheryl, Ricky, and Bobby Jr.—Barry grew up loving sports. He played them all, but baseball stood out above all others. And why not? After all, Barry learned the game from his father, who was a major-league All-Star for the San Francisco Giants.

Barry's childhood heroes included athletes Mickey Mantle, Kareem Abdul-Jabbar, Tony Dorsett, and Willie Mays. The legendary center fielder Mays was his favorite. Mays was Bobby Bonds's teammate, a good friend, and also Barry's godfather. Mays is among baseball's all-time leaders in runs, hits, runs batted in (RBIs), and home runs. Of course the stats didn't matter to young Barry—he just loved being around his godfather.

By the time Barry was two years old, he could hit a Wiffle

ball hard enough to shatter the glass in the living room windows. When he was three, his cousin Reggie Jackson became a major leaguer for the Kansas City Royals. At age four, Barry would regularly go to nearby Candlestick Park in San Francisco to watch his father's practices. At the ballpark, Barry and his little brother Ricky would play catch with Willie Mays on the outfield grass. As they got older, the two boys loved to shag (catch) fly balls during batting practice, to serve as batboys, and to hang out in the clubhouse with the pros after practice.

Barry Bonds comes from some pretty amazing lineage. Not only were his father and cousin Reggie Jackson skilled ballplayers, his uncle, Robert V. Bonds Jr., was drafted by the Kansas City Chiefs football team in 1965. In addition, his aunt, Rosie Bonds, was a member of the 1964 U.S. Olympic team and once held the women's national record in the 80-meter hurdles.

Barry displayed extraordinary talents as a youngster and had a real passion for the game at an early age. He soon became a star on his San Carlos Little League team. He enjoyed learning new things from the major leaguers at Candlestick Park and then showing the new moves to his teammates. One of his memories from youth baseball is playing rival Foster City in the title game. "We lost the championship," Barry recalled. "I wanted to win because I had a coach named Joe Garagebaldi who passed away, and we wanted to win it for him."

While young Barry honed his skills at home, his dad was on the road a lot. As a result, every moment he was around was precious to Barry. When Bobby was home, Barry loved to play pool with him in the family den. The game also instilled in Barry a strong desire to win: The winner got candy, while the loser had to do push-ups. "When I played with my dad, he was such a competitor, he couldn't lose," Barry recalled.

Bobby wanted to give his children as much time as he could and to teach them right and wrong. He figured that like many African American kids, they too might have to go through some adversity in their lives. So he wanted to prepare them for the upcoming challenges as best as he could. When Barry tasted his first bit of racism, Bobby wanted to make sure he didn't stoop to the level of his tormentors.

"I used to get in fights at school because I was black," recalled Barry. "I'll never forget, I came home one day and I said, 'I don't like white people right now.' . . . [My dad] said, 'Don't ever come in my house like that again. . . . Be proud of who you are. . . . Do not allow their stupidity to make you stupid.'"

After the 1974 baseball season, when Barry was ten years old, things changed considerably. He came home from school one day to learn that his father had been traded. Bobby would be playing for the New York Yankees. It would be the first of many trades for Bobby.

For Barry, the trade meant that he would see even less of his dad. The family traveled with Bobby when they could, but they remained in California so that the kids could continue at the same school. When Bobby was away, Pat Bonds held the family together. Barry said, "My mom was always there. . . . [She] did all the car pooling." She gave Barry the support he needed while also raising Cheryl, Ricky, and Bobby Jr.

BOBBY BONDS

Bobby Bonds (1946–2003) was an exciting player who had the rare ability to combine power with speed. He played a total of fourteen years in the major leagues, including seven with the Giants (1968–1974). A three-time All-Star, Bobby was a great defensive center fielder who won three Gold Gloves as well. He was the first man to have five seasons with at least thirty steals and thirty homers. "Know what I'm proudest of?" Bobby once said. "That now I'm known as Barry Bonds's father."

While not seeing his father much was tough on Barry, he became familiar with cities all across the United States, met famous ballplayers, and saw things that most kids his age had only read about. "I thought it was wonderful," said Barry. "I got a chance to travel around, see different cities like New York. I loved it."

At home, Barry also made the best of his situation. He did well in school and looked forward to playing sports. By the time he was in junior high school in the late 1970s, his talent put him head and shoulders above most of the other kids. Whatever the sport was, Barry wanted not only to succeed in it but to dominate it. His competitive nature and outstanding athletic ability were a recipe for success out on the ball field. Barry could throw, hit, and run as fast as kids much older than he was, and he had a real passion for the game. As a center fielder, Barry could cover a lot of ground in the outfield, tracking down pop flies with great speed and agility.

Of course, like all youngsters, Barry also spent time playing with other kids in the neighborhood. Bob McKercher, a neighborhood friend, remembered, "We were into water balloon fights. We played baseball, basketball, football. We loved music and liked to dance. We went to the movies. . . . [Barry] was just a typical kid."

In 1978, when Barry started at Serra High School, in the nearby suburb of San Mateo, his athletic skills continued to shine. Barry starred in baseball, basketball, and football. Even though he was the starting running back on the football team and a star guard on the basketball team, baseball remained his true love. Barry made the school's varsity baseball team as a sophomore and went on to hit .404 over his three-year career at Serra. He even managed to pull off a whopping .467 average his senior year. The center fielder also led the league in home runs, total bases, and stolen bases in each of his three years. In addition, Bonds led his team to three straight Central Coast Conference titles and was named to the all-city, all-league, and all-state teams each season.

❝ We just played baseball because it was fun. As long as you tried, it didn't matter. It didn't matter if you lost all the games. As long as you went out there and did your best. ❞

—BARRY BONDS DISCUSSING HIS HIGH SCHOOL YEARS

Barry's high school baseball coach, Dave Stevens, said, "Barry was a very easy young man to coach. An extremely hard worker. The year he hit .467, I remember if anyone was on base for us, teams would just walk him." According to Stevens, during a game against St. Francis High in Mountain View, Barry hit one homer more than 450 feet, and it wound up in a parking lot near the field. Another home run was nicknamed the "Bomb at the Beach." There, Barry crushed the ball, and it soared over the outfield wall and into some nearby sand dunes. Slamming balls that far takes tremendous strength, and most seventeen-year-olds can only dream of having the power to hit homers like that.

When Bobby was in town, he made an effort to attend Barry's games at Serra High. However, he rarely rooted for him from the stands. Instead, he would park his car behind some trees in the outfield and watch from there. He was a famous athlete, and he attracted a lot of attention wherever he went. He'd had his run-ins with the media over the years, and he valued his privacy. The last thing he wanted was to take away from Barry's time in the sun or to take the focus away from the kids on the ball field. It was tough sometimes to be the son of Bobby Bonds, a home-town superstar, but it made Barry try even harder to establish his own identity as a baseball player. Because Barry's dad was in the major leagues, everyone expected Barry to display superior skills from a very early age. Even the smallest mistake exposed him to serious criticism.

❝You don't know who your friends are at times. You don't know if [other kids] want to be your friends because you're the son of Bobby Bonds.**❞**

—BARRY BONDS

Barry recalled that his father constantly gave him advice

about how to improve his game. Bobby retired from professional baseball in 1981, giving him more time than ever to analyze his son's play. Barry noted, "One thing [my dad] especially didn't like was when I would get angry at striking out. He'd yell at me and say, 'Throwing down your helmet is not going to get you a hit.'"

Barry also had to learn to deal with the pressure of having Willie Mays and Reggie Jackson ready to critique his skills. Barry said, "Willie Mays kept his eye on me constantly and would often tell me I wasn't concentrating enough. Then there was Cousin Reggie, always ready to get his two cents in, too. One thing all three had in common: They would never accept excuses." Although it was tough to be so closely watched, Barry also benefited from the advice of such top-notch players.

In 1982, when Barry finished high school, he had established his reputation as a power hitter. During his senior year, professional baseball scouts came out in droves to watch him play. Many of them felt that Barry was ready to make the leap right into the major leagues. In professional baseball circles, some people guessed that he would be an early pick in the upcoming major-league draft, to be held in the summer of 1982. Others thought he might choose to go to college instead. The only person who knew for sure was Barry, and he had a lot of soul-searching to do before he could make such a big decision.

❝Most of the balls Barry hit were like they were shot out of bazookas. One of the first things I noticed about Barry was he had great balance at the plate and his swing was snap-of-your-fingers quick. You didn't have to do much fine-tuning.**❞**
—DAVE STEVENS, BARRY'S HIGH SCHOOL COACH

Shortly after graduating from high school, Barry was selected by the San Francisco Giants in the second round of the 1982 amateur draft. It was the opportunity of a lifetime to have the chance to play for the same team as his father. But even though Barry was happy, he also felt a little unsure about making the jump to the pros. Many of his friends from high school were going off to college. He felt confident that he would still be able to play in the major leagues in a few more years, and he didn't want to miss out on the college experience. When the Giants offered Barry a $70,000 contract, he told them he wanted more money. The Giants could see that Barry wasn't ready to sign, and they turned down his request.

With that decision out of the way, Barry had to decide where to go to college. He chose Arizona State University (ASU), one of the top baseball schools in the nation. "I told Barry that if he didn't feel ready yet . . . ASU would be a good place with good coaching," said his high school coach. Not only was it a college baseball power, it was also the school Reggie Jackson had attended. At ASU, Barry knew he could develop his skills and become a complete all-around baseball player. He also wanted to give himself the chance to let his hair down a bit and have some fun. He had the rest of his life to be a serious ballplayer.

"I just wanted to try to get to the next step," Barry later recalled. "That's why, when I got drafted out of high school, I wanted to go to college, because I thought if I could play at the next level with all the top athletes in that caliber, then I was ready for the next level. I never tried to jump too far ahead of myself."

Chapter Two

Sun Devil Sensation

In the fall of 1982, Barry was sad to leave home but anxious to begin the next chapter of his life at college. He arrived in Tempe, Arizona, with high expectations and didn't waste any time making a name for himself. He jumped right in as a freshman and tried to learn as much as possible—about his major, physical education, and about baseball. He was a scholarship athlete at ASU, which meant that he would be given free tuition in exchange for his services on the baseball diamond. Right away, Barry decided to honor Willie Mays by selecting number 24—Willie's old number—for his jersey. That would give Barry an extra boost of confidence to go out and play ball like a champion.

It wasn't always easy for Barry to fit in. Some of the other baseball players were jealous that he was so talented and that his dad was a major-league All-Star. A few of his teammates thought that he acted too cocky and arrogant. It was difficult for

Barry to be away from home, but he still made some good friends that year. He got through the hard times by focusing on baseball and trying to stay as positive as possible.

Although he enjoyed being with his friends at college, Barry spent a lot of time alone, out on the baseball diamond. He also made regular visits to the nearby spring-training facility of the Oakland Athletics (A's). At the training center, Barry worked out with A's All-Star outfielder Rickey Henderson, who was a friend of Bobby's. Rickey was well known for his amazing base-stealing abilities, and he offered to work with Barry on his baserunning techniques. Rickey showed Barry how to watch the pitcher's eyes to take advantage of any chance to get a good jump off first base and make a successful steal. Barry learned a lot from Rickey and applied that knowledge to make himself a better ballplayer at ASU.

With 1,406 stolen bases, All-Star center fielder Rickey Henderson is major-league baseball's all-time base-stealing champion. His major-league debut came in 1979 for the Oakland Athletics, and he has played for a number of other teams in his career.

By the end of his freshman year, Barry was thriving as a member of the Sun Devils. Under batting coach Jeff Pentland,

Barry sharpened his skills and learned to use his strength. He was lifting weights regularly, which gave him more power when he swung the bat. He led the team with eleven home runs and fifty-four RBIs his first season, and his confidence began to soar. Barry even went on to garner Most Valuable Player (MVP) honors at the 1983 West II Regional Tournament. During a tournament game against Brigham Young University, he hit a huge home run over ASU's center-field wall, nicknamed the "Green Monster."

At the end of the season, the Devils advanced to the College World Series, where Barry hit a pair of homers. The Devils beat the University of Maine and Oklahoma State University in the first and second rounds but then lost to the University of Alabama in the semifinals.

After his first year of college, Barry headed north to play summer baseball in the Alaskan League. He suited up for a team called the Goldpanners and lived in the city of Fairbanks. The Alaskan League was the top summer college baseball league at the time, and it attracted many of the best college players from around the country. Alaska was a great experience for Barry, who enjoyed getting away from it all and playing in the "Land of the Midnight Sun," as Alaska is often called.

In his sophomore season, Barry's summer training really paid off. He had six game-winning hits that year. Once again, he led the Sun Devils to the College World Series. There, he tied a College World Series record by rapping out seven consecutive hits. He was even named ESPN's amateur athlete of the week for his record-tying performance. The Devils were close to winning the 1984 championship but came up just short. After beating Washington State, Hawaii, and Stanford in the regionals, ASU advanced to the College World Series. They beat Miami 9–6 and Oklahoma State 23–12 but wound up falling to Texas 8–4 and Cal State Fullerton 6–1. Barry's season had come to an end.

By that time, Barry was the talk of college baseball. He finished the season with an impressive .360 batting average to go along with eleven home runs, thirty stolen bases, and fifty-five RBIs. In addition, Barry was named to the All-Pac-10 team, meaning he was the top center fielder of his conference, the Pac-10.

Barry sometimes enjoyed being in the limelight, and occasionally he performed amazing stunts on the field to impress the members of the media who followed him around. These stunts often gave Barry a reputation as someone who was arrogant and had a bad attitude. Barry, however, just thought it was fun. One instance involved Barry's challenging the team's pitching machine, which hurls high-speed balls at batters, during a practice. The incident was recalled by Richard Obert in the *Arizona Republic:* "It was starting to rain before the 1985 Arizona State alumni game at Packard Stadium, and a fearless kid named Barry Bonds was showing off to the big leaguers. Bonds, starting his junior season at ASU, stepped into a batting cage, and, with the pitching machine cranked at eighty-something [miles per hour], he moved closer and closer. Finally, Bonds was about thirty feet from the machine. Pitch. Whack. Pitch. Whack. Jaws dropped at the lightning in Bonds's aluminum bat."

As a junior, Barry belted out twenty-three home runs and emerged as one of the most respected leaders of his team. He was enjoying his experiences as a college student, and on the baseball diamond, his skills just kept improving. Barry was the anchor of a talented outfield that featured future major leaguers Oddibe McDowell in right field and Mike Devereaux in left field. Despite Barry's efforts, his team struggled at times. As a result, Arizona State ultimately came up short with a 31–35 record and missed qualifying for the regional tournament for the first time since 1982. There would be no postseason College World Series run this year for Barry and his teammates.

Even so, Barry had an awesome year, hitting .368, with twenty-three homers and sixty-six runs batted in. He made spectacular catches in the outfield and smashed home runs over the fence. For his efforts, he was again named a member of the All-Pac-10 team. To top it off, he was also named an

All-American, which meant that he was recognized as the top collegiate center fielder in the entire nation. It was the highest honor a college player could receive.

Baseball players can be drafted by professional teams immediately after high school graduation. If they decide to go to a four-year college, however, they cannot be drafted until the end of their third (junior) year of school.

At the end of Barry's junior year, he decided to leave school early and turn professional. He felt ready to pursue his lifelong dream of becoming a major leaguer. Arizona State was sad to see him go but was very proud of what he had accomplished. He finished his three-year career as a Sun Devil with a .347 batting average, 175 RBIs, and the third-most home runs in ASU history with forty-five. The school retired Barry's number 24 jersey.

Barry reentered the amateur draft in the summer of 1985. Because he had turned down the Giants' offer in 1982, he was again available to be drafted by the highest bidder. His performance in three years of college had made him attractive to even more teams. Many baseball scouts speculated that he would be chosen as the number one draft pick. Others felt that he was less desirable because of his reputation for having a bad attitude.

❝ *When you're a child and thinking about playing in the major leagues, just having that opportunity alone is special in itself. I thought having my number retired in college and having my name up there on the scoreboard at Serra High School was pretty special.*❞

—BARRY BONDS

Barry didn't care which team selected him. He was just ecstatic that he was finally going to be a big leaguer like his father.

Chapter | Three

Welcome to the Show

On June 3, 1985, Barry was selected by the Pittsburgh Pirates in the sixth overall pick of the first round of the major-league draft. He was excited about going to Pittsburgh, the Steel City, and about playing in the major leagues. As a kid, Barry had enjoyed watching former Pirate legends Roberto Clemente and Willie Stargell, and he couldn't wait to step onto the same ball field where they had played.

 Barry uses a thirty-four-inch, 31.5-ounce maple bat that is manufactured in Ottawa, Canada.

Barry reported to Pittsburgh later that week to meet and greet his new teammates as well as the local media. He also got to take a few swings in the batting cage at Three Rivers Stadium, the Pirates' home field, before being sent to the minor leagues. The Pirates' managers liked to give the new recruits a brief taste of what the big leagues were like. The managers knew that top players would make every effort to get back to that stadium.

THE PITTSBURGH PIRATES

The Pittsburgh Pirates were founded in 1887 as the Pittsburgh Alleghenies. They changed their name to the Pirates two years later after signing away a player from the Philadelphia Athletics. They participated in the first-ever World Series in 1903, losing to the Boston Americans. Since 1903 they have won the World Series five times.

Barry had quite a memorable experience during his first batting practice at Three Rivers Stadium. Coaches Jim Leyland and Don Zimmer watched from just behind the batting cage. In fifteen swings, he hit about ten balls out of the park. But he pulled all of them to right field, which was the natural way for a left-hander to hit. Leyland noted that it was easy to hit ball after ball to the same location. Barry overheard this comment, adjusted his swing to drive the next few pitches to left field, and finished by slamming one to center field. As the two coaches walked away, they were definitely impressed. Zimmer turned to Leyland and said, "What in the world are you doing sending this kid out [to the minor leagues]?"

After batting practice was over, it was down to the minors for Barry. His first stop was in Prince William, Virginia, where he played in the Class A Carolina League. Major-league baseball teams each have a system of minor-league teams, and most players must work their way up the system, gaining experience before appearing in the big leagues. Typically, a player first reports to the rookie league, followed by Class A, Class AA, and Class AAA. Barry was so good that he was able to skip rookie ball altogether and report directly for Class A. In the Carolina League, Barry immediately attracted notice both in the field and behind the plate. He was even named player of the month in July.

❝You fail seven out of ten times," said Barry of baseball's "standard of success," a .300 batting average. "I try to deliver 30 percent, with 100 percent effort. If I was in any other business—basketball, accounting, or the stock market—30 percent and I'd be out of a job. That's why you'll never see me get mad out there. I'm too grateful.❞

In Prince William, Barry also met a young slugger named Bobby Bonilla. Bonilla, a tough third baseman from New York City, was not drafted out of high school but was discovered by a Pirates scout while playing amateur baseball. He and Barry hit it off immediately and became good friends. They were both on the fast track to the big leagues and knew that if they worked hard, they would be playing alongside each other for the Pirates one day. Barry played well at Prince William, hitting .299, with thirteen homers and fifteen stolen bases in just seventy-one games before being called up to Class AAA Hawaii for the 1986 season.

Barry loved playing in Hawaii, but he didn't want to get too comfortable. After all, this was just another stop on his journey to get to the big leagues. He settled into a groove, however, hitting .311 in forty-four games. He led his team, the Hawaii Islanders, in home runs (13) and RBIs (37), and he was second on the team in stolen bases (16).

One day during batting practice, Pirates general manager Syd Thrift saw Barry hit a half dozen balls in a row over the right-field fence. Thrift joked with Barry and asked if he could hit that many homers over the left-field fence. Since Barry was a lefty, to hit balls left meant changing his swing, something that is very difficult for most players to do. Thrift wanted to see just how strong Barry was, and Barry responded by hitting five straight pitches into the left-field bleachers. He continued to play well and hoped that he would get his big break to play in the major leagues sometime soon.

The Pirates started the 1986 baseball season with six wins and two losses. Unfortunately, the team could not maintain that level of success. By the time Barry was called up, the team had a record of seventeen wins and twenty-four losses.

Barry finally got called up to "The Show," as the major leagues are called, on May 30, 1986, against the Dodgers at Three Rivers Stadium in Pittsburgh. He was thrilled to finally get his chance to make a name for himself. That night he played center field and batted seventh in the lineup. In his first at bat, Barry faced pitcher Orel Hershiser. He hit the ball, but it was a pop-up to the shortstop. From there he walked in the third, struck out in the fourth, lined out to the shortstop in the sixth, and struck out yet again in the ninth and eleventh innings of the extra-inning game. The Pirates lost 6–4, and Barry hadn't been able to give them any help. But he knew that he had to keep trying.

The following day, the Pirates faced the Dodgers again, and Bobby Bonds drove 120 miles from Cleveland, where he was working as a batting coach, to see the game. He watched with delight as Barry got his first hit, a double off of Rick Honeycutt.

At the beginning of Barry's career, reporters often compared him to his father. They also would accidentally call him by his father's name.

Just five days later, on June 4, in the fifth inning of a game at Atlanta–Fulton County Stadium, Barry faced the Atlanta Braves' right-handed pitcher Craig McMurtry. He slammed the ball for the first homer of his career. As the season progressed, Barry was full of confidence. In fact, when the New York Mets came to town that year and the press asked him how he felt about facing legendary pitcher Dwight Gooden, Barry replied, *"He's* going to have to face *me!"*

In Barry's first nine games, he had a solid .278 batting average with two homers and six RBIs. At that point, he fell victim to his first major-league batting slump, bringing his average down to .233. Rookies are especially vulnerable to slumps, but Barry felt added pressure because he was also racking up a high number of strikeouts at the plate. Bobby Bonds had set a major-league record for most strikeouts in a single season (189), and some baseball observers wondered whether Barry shared this trait in common with his father. Barry continued working closely with the team's batting coaches to adjust to the skill of major-league pitchers. In the meantime, he settled in with the older players on the team, who had started calling the twenty-two-year-old youngster "the Kid."

Bonds finished with a respectable rookie campaign, hitting .223, knocking out sixteen homers, driving in forty-eight RBIs, and stealing thirty-six bases in 113 games. Despite having missed the first two months of the major-league season, Barry led all of the major-league rookies in homers, RBIs, and stolen bases. On the flip side, Barry's Pirates finished in last place in the National League East Division, leaving the team with a lot of room for improvement.

Chapter Four

Most Valuable Player

That next season, Barry began the year in center field but wound up moving to left field to make room for newly acquired All-Star center fielder Andy Van Slyke. The move would prove to be a good one for Barry, and he has remained in left field ever since. In addition, Barry asked the team's management if he could switch his jersey from number 7, which he wore his rookie season, to number 24. It was a significant number for Barry—besides being Willie Mays's number, it was also his birth date. And it had brought him a lot of luck in college!

Bonds had a breakout season in 1987, becoming just the second player in Pirates history ever to reach the twenty-homer, twenty-stolen-base plateau. He was also playing well in his new outfield position. His best friend, Bobby Bonilla, was doing well, too, dividing his fielding time between third base and outfield.

Just when Barry thought things couldn't be any better, he faced one of the greatest power pitchers in history—Nolan Ryan. Barry was so in awe of Ryan that he actually struck out three times in a row, on nine straight pitches! It was a humbling experience for Bonds, who knew that he had to keep working hard to get better and better.

&&*He was very aggressive and took advantage of his running speed. He got on base and stole at will. He was a guy who you were always waiting for him to jump out and bite you and do exciting things and give you goose bumps.*&&
—LONGTIME PIRATES SCOUT ANGEL FIGUEROA IN 1987

By the end of the season, Bonds's average had climbed to .261. He had hit thirty-four doubles and twenty-five homers and scored ninety-nine runs. He also stole thirty-two bases, making him a scoring threat every time he got on base. Manager Jim Leyland moved Barry to the leadoff position, which meant that he would bat first in every game. This was a big honor, indicating the manager felt that Barry was skilled at getting on base in a high number of his at bats. That way, when the more powerful number three and four hitters got up, they could drive him in to score runs. "I put him in leadoff because most young players aren't ready to knock in runs; it's good experience for him," Leyland told ESPN's *SportsCentury.*

Barry also got his first real taste of the national media, who seemed to be very interested in nearly everything he was doing. Since he had a famous father *and* he was showing some talent of his own, the media were doubly interested. They wanted to know all about what Barry had learned from Bobby, Reggie Jackson, and Willie Mays. Barry later said, "I obviously appreciated their love and help, but it did leave me in a difficult position of being compared to all three. It seemed to me that the media thought I was competing with them." It didn't take long for Barry to get upset with the media for nosing into his business, so he figured he needed a strategy for dealing with them.

He talked with Leyland, who told him that he should focus on his game and not worry about the media. Leyland said, "You have to leave these reporters alone because these people are not your friends." In other words, the reporters were there to get stories—good or bad. Leyland also knew that Barry was a private person, so he warned him to be careful about what he told the reporters. Barry took his coach's advice seriously, and he began avoiding the media. As a result, sports reporters began to portray Barry in sometimes unflattering ways—calling him unfriendly, ungracious, and egotistical for not talking with them.

During Barry's busy second season as a Pirate, he managed to find enough time to fall in love. While he was in Montreal, Canada, he met a woman named Sun Branco. The two were engaged within just a few months. After the end of the 1987 season, the couple wed at a small ceremony in Las Vegas, Nevada. Barry had always wanted to have kids, and he was looking forward to starting a family with his new bride.

But before he knew it, the 1988 season was under way. Barry had another solid year, raising his average to .283 with twenty-four homers and fifty-eight RBIs. One of the season's highlights came on July 17, in a game against the San Francisco Giants. Jim Leyland had actually given Barry the day off to rest a sore knee, but when the team was tied late in the game, he asked Barry if he could pinch-hit to give his club a spark. Barry jumped up, grabbed a bat, and promptly crushed a Joe Price offering over the center-field fence to win the ball game. It's safe to say that was just the spark Leyland had been looking for!

Barry was still often compared to his father, but at least the press had good things to talk about. "He attacks the ball just the same way his dad did," said longtime Cardinals broadcaster Mike Shannon. "It's got to be tough playing under the shadow of his dad. But he doesn't let it bother him. He's got a lot of guts just to be out there."

Bobby Jr.

Bobby Bonds Jr., Barry's younger brother, went on to play baseball as a left fielder at Canada College in Redwood City, Canada. Afterward he was drafted by the San Diego Padres in the eighteenth round of the 1992 draft. He played minor-league ball for the Padres from 1992 to 1995 before moving over to play for the Giants' minor-league teams from 1996 to 1998. Twice he made it as high as the AAA level, but he never made it to the majors.

Perhaps the highlight of the season came in mid-August in a game against the Philadelphia Phillies. As part of the festivities that day, an old-timers game was held before the matchup. It was a wonderful reunion as Barry got to watch his father put on his old Giants uniform and even slap out a home run. Not to be outdone, Barry hit two homers of his own in the game to drive in five runs as he led Pittsburgh to a 10–4 win. After the game, Barry said, "Having my father around is an inspiration and his presence gets me going and gets my blood flowing. If I have days like this every time he's around, I'll pay for him to come with me everywhere."

Barry's numbers dipped in 1989, and his average fell to .248. He hit just nineteen homers and drove in fifty-eight RBIs.

Was Barry in a slump? Were the pressures of marriage and being in the limelight taking their toll? Was the media hounding him also having an effect? Barry's behavior during games—which some viewed as "showing off"—put more strain on his relationship with the media. He often caught fly balls out in the outfield with only one hand (instead of two), he slowly jogged around the bases when he hit a home run instead of running, and he sometimes slapped his glove on his chest in an arrogant manner just before catching a pop fly. Reporters preferred players who came across as modest and friendly—not overconfident and aloof.

"I feel the press puts a stamp on certain players, and once they stamp you as a 'bad person,' then that's what they feed on and there's nothing you can do about it," Bonds said. "I know in my heart the type of ballplayer I am and the type of person I am."

Barry trained like a madman that off-season alongside his buddy Bobby Bonilla, lifting weights, running, and spending hours upon hours in the batting cage. Since both were stars in the national spotlight, they helped each other deal with the pressure they faced. They figured that instead of them talking to the media, they would let their bats do the talking for them.

Then on December 18, 1989, Barry and Sun became the proud parents of a baby boy named Nikolai. With his little son watching, Barry saw his efforts pay off in the 1990 season as he emerged as a superstar. Barry came out and hit .301, with thirty-three home runs, 114 RBIs, 104 runs scored, fifty-two stolen bases, and a league-leading .565 slugging average. (A player's slugging percentage is the number of total bases he accumulates per at bat.)

That year Barry was proud to be named to the National League All-Star team for the first time. He even joined Cincinnati's Eric Davis as the second player in major-league history to hit thirty homers and steal fifty bases in a season. Barry also displayed stellar fielding, throwing out fourteen base runners from left field. The strength of his arm would make the rest of the league think twice about trying to take an extra base off him.

The Pirates as a whole had a strong season, and many observers thought the team had gotten a boost when Leyland moved Barry from the leadoff spot to number three, four, or five in the batting order. Barry was moved because he'd emerged as a power hitter, capable of hitting a lot of home runs. With his new position, when he came up to bat, there were more runners in scoring position who could make it home on one of his long hits. This change gave Barry the opportunity to drive in many more runs, and the team benefited. Barry had lobbied for the move for some time, but Leyland wanted to make sure he was ready for the challenge of being expected to consistently hit with power.

By the time the regular season had concluded, Barry and the Pirates had reached the postseason play-offs. For their first game, they squared off against the Cincinnati Reds in the National League Championship Series (NLCS). Barry struggled in his first NLCS, however, going just three for eighteen (.167), with no home runs and only one RBI. In fact, the entire Pirates lineup struggled as Van Slyke and Bonilla also had problems at the plate. Collectively, the trio batted just .190. With such poor batting, the team couldn't pull off the series. Even so, the games were tight and the margin of defeat in Pittsburgh's four losses was just seven runs.

❝*I want to be up in that [clutch] situation to have a shot at it, but I don't have dreams about the World Series or having the bases loaded. . . . My dreams are [that we're ahead] 9–0 and we're winning in the World Series rather than having a situation where there's a noose around my neck. I try to look at things a little easier than stressful.*❞

—BARRY BONDS ON PRESSURE

Barry was disappointed about losing in the play-offs, but his mood improved when the year's awards were handed out and he was named by the Baseball Writers America Association as National League MVP. Incredibly, his buddy and teammate Bobby Bonilla finished as the MVP runner-up. Barry had become the first player ever to average .300, hit thirty homers, drive in 100 runs, and steal fifty bases in a single season. In addition, Barry also won his first Gold Glove award, which is an honor given to baseball's top defensive player at each position. Even though he had a difficult relationship with the writers, it was clear that they still found his combination of offensive and defensive skills unparalleled.

"I think I had an MVP season," said Barry. "This was just an unreal year. I don't know if I can ever do this again, but I can tell my kids and grandkids that for six months I was up there with the best of them."

That off-season, Barry and Sun welcomed their second child, Shikari, into their lives. It wasn't all rosy for Barry in Pittsburgh, though. The media continued to hound him. They wanted to know what made him tick. They wanted to know what this MVP did in his spare time. They wanted to know about his wife and children. They wanted to know about his relationships with his father and godfather. They even wanted to know what he did when he went out at night with his buddies. It was, at times, too much to take. He was a young man who had watched his father go through the same torment with the press as a child and was determined not to let it happen again.

Chapter Five

Postseason Problems

As 1991 spring training approached, Barry asked to renegotiate his contract with the Pirates. Since he had won the league's MVP award, he felt that he deserved a higher salary. When he asked for $3.2 million per year, however, many in the press, along with many Pirates fans, criticized him for being greedy. The Pirates also thought that the amount was too high, and they gave him $2.3 million. The strain of the negotiations and the media's harsh reaction put Barry under even more pressure.

During spring training in Florida, one incident in particular put Barry over the edge. It involved some cameramen who were trying to film Barry while he was practicing drills on the field. Even though the cameramen had permission from the team to be there, Barry wasn't in the mood to be filmed, and he told them to leave. When they didn't leave, Barry became angry and began yelling at them. The commotion attracted other players and coaches on the field, and finally Leyland came over to straighten things out. Leyland was furious that one of his players was behaving in such a disrespectful manner toward the press and toward the other coaches who had tried to calm him down.

Stories of Barry's outburst made him even less popular with baseball fans. During a preseason game against the Boston Red Sox, the crowd booed when Barry was introduced. They booed again when he caught a fly ball in the outfield but finally cheered when he hit a two-run homer out of the park. After the game, Barry told reporters that the booing just made him play harder.

CONFIDENCE

When asked what he felt was the most important aspect for becoming a good hitter, Barry said it all had to do with confidence. "You have to challenge yourself, and you have to beat the fear inside of your body. . . . Once you over-come your fear and you build your confidence, then you've accomplished a lot."

As the season got under way, Barry was determined to prove that his numbers from the previous season were no fluke. He produced impressive stats that year, though not the MVP-type numbers of the year before. He finished with a .292 average, knocked out twenty-five homers, drove in 116 RBIs, scored ninety-five runs, and stole forty-three bases. He won his second Gold Glove award as well. More importantly, Barry led his club back to the play-offs, where the twenty-seven-year-old outfielder was determined to step up his game.

Unfortunately, Barry's second NLCS wound up being worse than the first, and he recorded just four hits in twenty-seven at bats (.148), with no home runs or RBIs. Pittsburgh battled to the very end against the Atlanta Braves. The Pirates led the Braves 3–2 after five games, but they lost game six in the ninth inning, 1–0. Having also lost their momentum, the Pirates got shut out in game seven to end the series. It was a very difficult way for Barry to end the year. He desperately wanted his team to win, and he was angry that he was unable to do more to see that happen.

In 1992 Barry came out swinging for the fences and never looked back. He was determined to play well despite the fact that Bobby Bonilla, his best friend and teammate, had left the Pirates to sign with the New York Mets. Barry and Bobby had formed a powerful tandem that Pittsburgh sportswriters dubbed the "BB Gunners." In Bonilla's five full seasons with the Pirates, he was a four-time All-Star.

With Bonilla gone to the Big Apple, Barry carried the load for his team that year. He was sad that his friend had left, but he still tried to play as hard as he could. With Bobby gone, however, it seemed that all of the media attention now fell onto his shoulders. Reporters were especially interested in Barry's plans for the future. He was a free agent after 1992, so it was possible that he was in his final year in Pittsburgh. Early in the season, Barry indicated that he would definitely consider leaving to join a new team, though he also made some positive comments about the Pirates. He stated that the amount of money offered by various teams would be a factor in his decision. Some in the media thought Barry's statements showed that he was a disloyal player who only cared about money.

Barry's hobbies include weight lifting, golf, martial arts, dancing, and computers. He even cofounded Digital Interiors, Inc., a San Jose–based electronics company that installs state-of-the-art technology in homes. Barry loves fiddling with the latest gadgets and has his house wired with eight computers and nineteen televisions.

Once Barry and his teammates took the field, they were all business. They started off with a bang—by the end of the first two weeks, the Pirates had a 9–2 record and were riding high on a six-game winning streak. In mid-June, Barry strained a muscle in his rib cage and was placed briefly on the disabled list for the first time in his major-league career. He didn't let the injury slow him down for long, though, and by the All-Star break in mid-July, Barry was batting .303 and had tallied fifteen homers. The team continued playing well after the break, and in late August they were ranked first in their division, followed closely by Montreal. On September 27, they won their third-straight NL East Division championship by beating the New York Mets 4–2.

---

66 *My goal is to win a World Series because that's a team thing. Your biggest goal as an individual is probably to go to the Hall of Fame. That's the highest standard in baseball. . . . For the rest of your life, people are going to walk through this museum and have the opportunity to read history or know about [these] people forever. I think that's the greatest feat as an individual. As a team, it's the World Series, because it takes everyone to do that.* 99

—BARRY BONDS

The Pirates were back in the play-offs! Barry had also put up his finest numbers to date. He posted a .311 batting average, hit thirty-four homers, drove in 103 RBIs, scored 109 runs, and stole thirty-nine bases—his second 30-30 season (he hit at least thirty homers and stole at least thirty bases). He was such a threat that opposing teams walked him a league-leading 127 times. His power and on-base numbers were amazing. And if that wasn't enough, Barry had solidified himself as the best defensive left fielder in the game as well, winning his third straight Gold Glove award.

Despite Barry's outstanding individual numbers in 1992, his play-off nightmares continued. The Pirates were once again up against the Atlanta Braves. Trailing 3–1 after four games, the Pirates roared back to pound Atlanta in games five and six. After the first half of the ninth inning in game seven, Pittsburgh was ahead 2–0. But in the bottom of the ninth, the Braves rallied. Atlanta scored one run early in the inning. Then, with the bases loaded and two outs, Atlanta sent up Francisco Cabrera to pinch-hit. Cabrera drilled a single to Barry out in left field. Barry charged the ball and heaved it to home plate. Meanwhile, David Justice scored to tie the game, and Sid Bream was chugging around third base as the winning run. Barry's throw got there just in time for Pirates catcher Mike LaValliere to tag Bream as he was sliding into home. It was almost too close to call, but in the end the umpire signaled that he was safe. The Atlanta fans mobbed the field in celebration while Barry sat helplessly on the ground in left field wondering why his team just couldn't make it past the NLCS. The loss was the team's worst heartbreak yet.

Barry was beside himself. He had stepped it up this time, going six for twenty-three (.261 average), with one home run and two RBIs, but still found himself out of the World Series for the third straight year. The media had come up with a theory that Bonds was a choker in the play-offs. They said that Barry couldn't win the big one to get his team into the World Series. It was a nasty slam against the game's best player, and it made Barry want to win more than ever.

"It does affect you," said Bonds in an interview. "You're human. How can you be so good and do so well in 162 games and then all of a sudden disappear? You feel like you've disappeared. All of a sudden now I'm this ghost, I'm gone."

Shortly after the loss, Barry did get some good news. He was awarded his second MVP, making him just the tenth player in baseball history to win more than one National League MVP. "I want to do it again," he said confidently. "I'm twenty-eight. I want to be the first to do it four times."

Chapter Six

Coming Home

After the 1992 season ended, Barry became a free agent. His contract was up with Pittsburgh, and he felt that as one of the game's elite players, he should be paid as such. The Pirates couldn't afford to keep him, so they didn't even offer him a new contract. As a result, Barry was free to go to the highest bidder. The New York Yankees offered him a five-year, $36 million contract, but he turned it down. On December 8, 1992, Barry reached a deal with the San Francisco Giants. His six-year, $43.75 million contract made him the highest-paid baseball player of all time.

Best of all, Barry was heading home and joining Bobby's old team. In interviews he said, "It's like a boyhood dream that came true for me. All I've ever wanted to do is share something with my father. This is the greatest moment in my entire life." To make it even sweeter, that following week, Barry's dad was named as the new hitting coach of the Giants. It would be like old times, with father and son playing ball together at Candlestick Park.

To top it all off, Dusty Baker was named as the team's new manager. Bobby and Dusty were longtime friends and had even gone to elementary school together. Barry, Bobby, and Dusty were ready to take San Francisco by storm!

❞*Every time I step on that field, I know my godfather's in center field and my dad's in right field.*❟
—BARRY BONDS, AFTER SIGNING HIS CONTRACT
WITH THE GIANTS

When Barry came on board, the Giants had just been saved from a possible move to Florida. They needed to rebuild their San Francisco Bay Area fan support. Barry's presence, in addition to attracting more fans, would also help the team's owners raise enough money to build a new stadium. Even though Candlestick Park had a great history behind it, the franchise needed a new stadium to generate more revenue. A new, state-of-the-art stadium would increase fan interest and ticket sales. With more money, the team could afford to pay higher salaries to better players. With better players, the team would have a stronger shot at winning the World Series. In addition,

Candlestick Park was notoriously cold because of the angle at which winds blew in from San Francisco Bay. Fans knew to pack extra clothing anytime they wanted to attend a game.

Candlestick Park is so windy that during the 1961 All-Star game, a large gust actually blew Stu Miller right off the pitcher's mound!

Barry came to San Francisco with all the hype and fanfare of a rock star. The media had pegged him as the savior of the franchise. It would be a lot of pressure for Barry to handle, but that was why he was getting paid the big bucks.

"If you ask me, he's a bargain," said former Giant Jeff Brantley. "He can pretty much do it all. His baseball instincts are unbelievable. And he's not just trying to get a hit, he's trying to crush the ball. If you make a bad pitch, he'll hit a home run and he'll embarrass you."

When Bonds arrived in San Francisco, his first request was to unretire his godfather's number 24 jersey. Old-time Giants fans were not happy about this request. Willie Mays had been a first-class player, and they felt that to bring back his number would be a sign of disrespect. In the end, Barry agreed to wear 25, his father's old number, instead.

WILLIE MAYS

Willie Mays was arguably the greatest ballplayer ever to play the game. He combined power, speed, and grace on the diamond in ways that were unheard of before his time. Mays played in the major leagues for more than two decades and spent twenty-one seasons with the Giants. He was the first player ever to hit fifty home runs and steal twenty bases in a single season. When he retired in 1973, Mays ranked third in career home runs, with 660.

After spring training, the team opened its schedule on the road. As luck would have it, they faced the Pirates on April 9, 1993. On that day, Barry returned to Pittsburgh for the first time since signing with the Giants. He was booed unmercifully, and some upset fans even threw phony dollar bills onto the field to let him know that they weren't pleased with his decision to leave them for more money. Barry let his bat do his talking and responded appropriately by hitting a double and a triple and scoring three runs. Unfortunately, the Giants still lost 6–5.

Three nights later, some 56,689 fans, the largest regular-season crowd in San Francisco history, came out to see Bonds's home debut. Just before the start of the game, the Giants held a brief ceremony to honor Barry. Willie Mays, along with pop singer Michael Bolton, a friend of Barry's, gathered around home plate to present him with the league MVP trophy that he had won in 1992. The crowd went wild.

> The Giants franchise began as the New York Gothams in 1883. Two years later, the team was renamed the Giants. The team was a fixture in New York City until 1958, when it moved west to San Francisco. Once dominant, the Giants played in a World Series in six of the first seven decades of the twentieth century. The Giants have won more baseball games than any other major-league franchise in history, and only the New York Yankees have won a larger percentage of their games.

And how would Barry respond to being the new star in Candlestick Park that night? The slugger came out and smacked a towering homer in his first at bat. Things just kept rolling from there as he got the fans excited about Giants baseball again. In April, Barry hit a red-hot .431 and was named player of the month. The team won twenty-four of their first forty games and seemed to be on a roll by midseason.

At the midway point of the year, Barry was the leading vote getter for the All-Star game. He didn't disappoint in that appearance, either. He led the charge for the National League squad with a pair of doubles. By then everyone seemed to want to know the secret to his success. "I just know the game well, I guess," said Barry. "I don't try to evaluate every little thing that other people are doing. I just try to keep myself mechanically sound. . . . If I'm mechanically sound, it doesn't really make a difference what [the pitchers] throw."

Barry's club played great baseball that season, winning a team record 103 ball games. The Giants had been in first place in the National League West for nearly the entire season, but with two months left, the defending National League champion Atlanta Braves started gaining ground. Those same pesky Braves who had caused Barry so much grief in Pittsburgh were at it again.

Barry tried to step up his game, hitting six homers and driving in twenty-one RBIs in the final sixteen games. It all came down to the last game of the season, with the Giants facing the Dodgers in Los Angeles. If the Giants could win this game, they would make the play-offs; if not, Atlanta would. It did not go well that day, as Mike Piazza and the Dodgers crushed San Francisco 12–1. San Francisco was out of the play-offs and done for the season.

Despite his team's season-ending meltdown, Barry had pulled off another outstanding individual season. In fact, he became just the seventh player in major-league history to win the MVP award three times. His numbers were amazing—he had finished the 1993 season with a .336 batting average. It was twenty-five points higher than his previous best average of .311. He also topped the National League with forty-six home runs and 123 RBIs. His slugging percentage of .677 was the highest since Mickey Mantle's in 1961. Barry also collected yet another Gold Glove award—his fourth—showing why he was the best all-around player in baseball.

SUPERSTAR BARRY

In addition to Barry's many accolades on the field, he has acquired a few special ones off the field. Among them are being named one of *People* magazine's "50 Most Beautiful People in the World" and one of *People*'s "25 Most Intriguing People." He has also made his mark in Hollywood, having guest starred in episodes of *Beverly Hills 90210, Arli$$, Everybody Loves Raymond,* and *Nash Bridges.* He even appeared as himself in the 1993 baseball movie *Rookie of the Year.*

After the end of the season, Giants owner Peter Magowan seemed to think that the money spent on Barry had been a good investment. "He truly loves to play," said Magowan. "In one game, he made a game-saving catch and cut three sure doubles off at the line and held them to singles; in a couple of cases, his plays saved what would have been runs. He's made everyone in the field more aggressive. . . . Barry has dramatically affected the way the Giants play the game."

That off-season, Barry worked harder than ever on every aspect of his game. He even tried out a new drill that tested his eyesight in a unique way. A hitting instructor would pitch balls to him with numbers written on them. Barry would have to swing at only certain numbered balls, which the instructor would call out while they were in midair. This forced him to watch the ball very closely and study its spin very quickly to see if it was the right number to hit. The drill worked well, and Barry again put up some pretty incredible numbers in the next season.

Before the 1994 baseball season began, the Giants redesigned their uniforms. The front of the home jersey displayed the word Giants in block-style letters and the away jersey spelled out the words San Francisco (rather than SF), matching the style of uniforms that Willie Mays and his teammates wore in 1958.

The 1994 season had a lot of ups and downs. Sandwiched between All-Stars Matt Williams and Darryl Strawberry, Barry had settled into a groove in the lineup. Barry's spot in the batting order meant that pitchers couldn't pitch around him. In the past, if the batter after Barry wasn't very good, then the pitcher could just walk Barry, figuring that the next guy would be much easier to get out. The trio was awesome at the plate, taking turns driving in each other and putting a lot of numbers up on the board. The team started out with a strong 5–2 record and then evened out to 12–12 by May 1. But unfortunately, by the end of June they were 33–46 and slumping.

Barry has won a total of four ESPY awards, presented by the all-sports TV channel ESPN. The awards, which have been dubbed the "Oscars of Sports," are voted on by the fans and awarded in an annual ceremony. In 1994 Barry won a pair of ESPYs for the categories Outstanding Baseball Performer and Male Athlete of the Year.

One of the year's highlights came on August 2, when Barry had his first three-homer game of his career in a 9–7 loss to the Cincinnati Reds. With two months remaining in the season,

Barry was again posting huge numbers: thirty-seven home runs, eighty-one RBIs, and twenty-nine stolen bases. Reporters speculated that he might even become the second player in major-league history to reach the 40-40 mark (forty homers and forty stolen bases) by the end of the season. His Giants had gotten back on track. Matt Williams was on pace to break Roger Maris's thirty-three-year-old record of sixty-one homers in a single season. The Giants were just three games behind the rival Dodgers in the standings and poised to make a run for the division lead. The team was playing well toward late summer, and by August 10, they had rallied back to a 55–60 record. Then everything came to a screeching halt.

The baseball owners and players union couldn't reach a new salary agreement, so the players went on strike. The players wanted more money and more benefits, and the owners wanted to set a salary cap (maximum). Owners had noticed that teams based in larger cities could sell more tickets, which generated more money. Most of the owners thought it wasn't fair that these wealthy teams could afford more talented players than the rest of the league. The owners wanted to make the situation more equal by allowing teams to share profits with one another and by setting limits on how much money players could earn.

As a result, the season was cut short and the World Series was canceled. It was a disaster all around, and the fans were furious. To make matters even worse for Barry, that December he and Sun went through a divorce. They did decide, however, to share custody of their two children. Nikolai and Shikari were the one bright spot in Barry's long, bleak off-season.

Chapter | Seven

Another Try

Barry again worked hard that spring and focused on the fundamentals. When the team reported for preseason training, he was ready to play ball. The Giants started out slowly in 1995, but Barry shouldered the load for his teammates when they were down. During one amazing stretch in July, Barry swatted three dramatic game-winning home runs to keep his ball club in the thick of things. The first came against the San Diego Padres when he launched a three-run bomb in the bottom of the ninth for a 7–6 win. The next victims were the Cincinnati Reds, when Barry's solo homer gave the Giants an 8–7 victory. He followed that up the next night with a three-run dinger in the ninth, this time giving his Giants a thrilling 7–5 win.

San Francisco played cat and mouse with their rival the Colorado Rockies that year, getting to within just a few games of first place on a couple of occasions. But when Giants cleanup hitter Matt Williams suffered a broken foot midway through the season, it spelled trouble. Barry tried to carry the load by himself but just couldn't keep up. With Williams out of the lineup, opposing teams pitched around Barry, seldom giving him any good pitches to hit. They preferred to walk Barry rather than give him a chance to send another ball out of the park. As a result, Barry wound up leading the league with 120 walks. And worst of all, the Giants finished the 1995 season in last place by eleven games.

Despite the team's drop in the standings that year, Barry still found a way to make history. He racked up thirty-three home runs and thirty-one stolen bases. It was the third time Barry had reached the coveted 30-30 plateau. However, it was the first time a San Francisco Giant had accomplished the feat in more than two decades. The last Giant to reach the mark was none other than Bobby Bonds. "Whenever we talk on the phone, Barry knows I've been there," said Bobby. "There's no situation that comes up for Barry that I haven't gone through myself."

Many in the media began to question whether or not it was possible for Barry to go from 30-30 to 50-50. "If I ever did try to do that, I'd hit about .220," joked Barry. "You'd have to be willing to give up something for it and I'm not willing to give up anything. I like the 30-30 and hitting .300 and driving in 100 and scoring 100. To me, that's as complete as you can be."

Even though Barry didn't want to aim for 50-50, he still set high goals for himself. He kicked off the 1996 season in style by belting his 300th career home run against Florida pitcher John Burkett. The homer put him in a very exclusive fraternity. He joined his dad, Willie Mays, and Chicago Cubs great Andre Dawson as the only players in major-league baseball history to hit 300 home runs and steal 300 bases. Said Barry afterward, "It's a good feeling, but I've got another record of my own: 400-400."

Bonds played hard, but he suffered a setback at the end of the summer. On August 25, Barry's franchise record of 357 consecutive games played ended when he suffered a hamstring injury. Incredibly, it was the second-longest consecutive game streak among current major league players, putting Barry behind only Cal Ripken Jr.

Barry took care of his body and made a quick recovery. On September 27, he became the second player in major-league history to hit forty homers and steal forty bases in a season. His blazing speed coupled with the fact that he reached base so much, via walks or by hits, made him a real scoring threat. Barry went from being "Mr. 30-30" to "Mr. 40-40." Jose Canseco had been the only other player to accomplish this feat. It was a disappointing season for the Giants, though, and they again finished in the cellar of the NL West.

As Barry got older—he turned thirty-two in 1996—he knew he had to work even harder to stay in shape. He became a work-out machine, training and conditioning five days a week under the supervision of personal trainer Raymond Farriss. Farriss, who also tutored football stars Jerry Rice and Roger Craig, was amazed at Barry's athletic abilities. He instructed him in running, sprints, lifting weights, and stretching. In just four months of training, Barry lowered his body fat from 12 percent to 8 percent, and he bulked up his bench press from 230 to 315. He came to camp in the spring of 1997 with a lot more flexibility. At six-foot two and 228 pounds, Barry was an intimidating opponent.

In a home run derby at the 1996 All-Star game, Barry Bonds beat Mark McGwire 3–2 in the final round. He hit seventeen homers in the contest to beat out every other competitor.

Reporters wanted to know what had happened to Barry. "I thought I was in great shape the way I worked out before because I was putting up the numbers I did, but I was out of shape," he told them. "I wanted to prove to myself that I could do it, and I'm happy with the results, but it doesn't guarantee success."

Barry starred in football, basketball, and baseball while playing for the Serra Padres.

Barry's hitting and fielding skills improved during his three years at Arizona State University.

Barry made a name for himself and won his first two MVP awards while playing for the Pittsburgh Pirates.

After his 1999 elbow surgery, Barry began wearing an arm brace to protect his right arm from stray pitches.

The whole family at Pac Bell Park—Barry and his wife, Liz, sit behind *(left to right)* Nikolai, Aisha, and Shikari.

In April 2001, Barry celebrated his 500th home run with two Giants heroes, Willie McCovey *(left)* and Willie Mays *(right)*.

On October 5, 2001, Barry thrilled fans and sealed his place in home-run history by hitting his seventy-second homer of the season.

Barry has had to learn how to handle the swarms of reporters that crowd him after games.

© Getty Images/Getty Images

© Sportschrome East/West, Rob Tringali

Barry slams out a homer off of Anaheim Angels pitcher Francisco Rodriguez in game six of the 2002 World Series. It was his fourth homer of the series.

Barry, an eight-time Gold Glove award winner, stands ready to grab anything that comes his way. Behind him, a sign honors his career record of more than 500 home runs and 500 stolen bases.

Barry's dramatic change caused some writers and fans to wonder whether he was on steroids. Barry, who prided himself on how much he trained, actually took the accusations as a compliment on all his hard work. He knew he didn't take steroids, and that was enough for him. He simply didn't feel that he had to dignify the question with a response.

By the end of the 1997 season, Barry hit an impressive .291, swatted forty homers, drove in 101 runs, stole thirty-seven bases, and once again led the league in walks, with 145. It was his fifth 30-30 season, tying his father's major-league record. To top it all off, Barry stepped up his game at the end of the season and helped carry his team back into the postseason for the first time since 1989. The worst-to-first Giants were back in the thick of things, and Barry was leading the charge.

Barry had high hopes that this would be the year his team would finally go all the way to the World Series. But the Giants bullpen fell apart in the National League Division Series against the Florida Marlins. The Giants pitchers weren't able to preserve a couple of solid leads. Barry managed to crank out three hits and two RBIs in the series but couldn't produce any long balls to help his team. The upstart Marlins swept the Giants in three straight games and would eventually become the unlikely champions of baseball. It was a huge upset, and the fans were shocked. It was a sad ending to yet another good year. Unfortunately, the loss only solidified Barry's reputation as a postseason bust. "Now I've probably figured out why I don't hit in the play-offs," admitted Bonds. "The spotlight . . . it's tough."

Barry got remarried before the 1998 season to longtime friend Elizabeth Watson. During the reception, Barry even serenaded his bride in front of some 240 guests, singing the song "My, My, My" by R&B singer Johnny Gill.

Barry had a strong regular season in 1998. He hit .303, with thirty-seven homers, 122 RBIs, and twenty-eight stolen bases. In his eighth All-Star appearance, he hit his first midsummer classic home run—a three-run shot off of Cleveland's Bartolo Colon. On August 23, Barry quietly hit his 400th career homer off of Marlins righty Kirt Ojala. With it came the distinction of becoming the first and only player in major-league baseball history to hit 400 home runs and steal 400 bases. "I don't think people realize what a great feat this is," Giants manager Dusty Baker said. "It's a combination of speed, power, and durability. To run that much and hit that much, you've got to be in tremendous shape for a long time."

The main baseball event of the year had nothing to do with Barry, however. It seemed that the entire nation was glued to the epic race between Mark McGwire and Sammy Sosa to top Roger Maris's single-season home run record. In 1961 Maris had hit sixty-one homers. McGwire and Sosa were both on pace to shatter that record.

As the summer came to a close, much of the usual media attention was diverted from Barry. He played his best baseball of the season in August and September, hitting an impressive .364 and again putting his Giants in a position to get back into the play-offs. He also set a National League record during a stretch in early September by reaching base safely in fifteen straight plate appearances. Over that amazing span of four games, he went nine for nine with six walks. By the end of the season, the team was deadlocked with the Chicago Cubs for the wild-card play-off spot. The Giants and the Cubs were forced to play a one-game play-off on the last day of the season for the right to advance to the division play-offs. This one wasn't meant to be, however, as the Giants came up short and ended their season on a downer yet again. It was more of the same for Barry, whose frustration continued. After the game, he simply didn't want to speak to the media about his team's play-off futility.

But Barry had his family to distract him and help him through the off-season. In February 1999, he and his wife, Liz, rejoiced when Liz gave birth to a baby girl they named Aisha.

Early in the 1999 season, Barry's age started to catch up with him. For just the second time in his thirteen-year career, he found himself on the disabled list. He needed surgery to remove a bone spur in his elbow and to repair a damaged triceps tendon in his left arm. As a result, he missed most of the first half of the season—nearly fifty games. When he was finally able to play again, he jumped back into the action.

On June 27, Barry got the ultimate show of respect when he passed the legendary Hank Aaron for most career intentional walks, with 293. Then on September 11, Bonds spanked out a double against Atlanta's Tom Glavine to give him 2,000 hits for his major-league career. Barry ended the season by hitting thirty-four homers and eighty-three RBIs in just 104 games. But Barry had come back too late for the Giants to recover from their time without him. The team had won just twenty-five games and lost twenty-two in his absence. They wound up missing the play-offs once again.

That off-season Barry had surgery on his right knee. Although Barry was getting older, manager Dusty Baker said he still had confidence in his abilities on the field. "As long as Barry continues to love the game, he'll be great," said Baker. "I believe as most guys get older, it's not the body, it's if you continue to love the game the same. I do believe he loves the game."

In the summer of 1999, *Sporting News* named Barry as the "Player of the Decade" for the 1990s. In a ten-year span, Barry had won three MVPs, had earned eight Gold Gloves, and was ranked in the top three in home runs, RBIs, slugging percentage, and walks.

Barry came out with a renewed sense of purpose in the 2000 season, thanks in large part to the beautiful new stadium, called Pacific Bell Park, that was built for the Giants. The new stadium had it all, including a bay-front view overlooking the Pacific Ocean. Barry could hardly wait to start launching homers into "McCovey Cove" (named for Giants great Willie McCovey), where fans would wait to retrieve home run balls in their canoes and kayaks.

Thirty-six-year-old Barry made a slight change in his training routine. On the advice of his father, Barry focused more on stretching and flexibility rather than on weight lifting and power. As he got older, he was concerned about becoming too bulky. He wanted to keep his body quick and lean. The results were awesome as Barry reemerged as one of the best hitters in baseball, setting career highs in home runs with forty-nine and a .688 slugging percentage. He poured it on down the stretch as well, posting a career-best fourteen-game hitting streak in September with a .426 batting average. Despite his amazing numbers, Barry finished second in the MVP race to his teammate Jeff Kent, who hit an impressive .334 with thirty-three home runs and 125 RBIs.

Behind Bonds and Kent, the Giants rolled to the best record in the National League and made it back to the postseason. This time they met up with the New York Mets in the National League Division Series. Barry went just three for seventeen, however, with no homers and only one RBI as the Giants lost the series, three games to one.

"Every year I go through a long season and I get close to a championship, and every year I go home disappointed," said Bonds. "Every year I have to go back to the drawing board and figure out what am I doing wrong or what are we doing wrong as a team. We're all going home thinking, I wish I was still playing, I wish I was in the World Series. I get tired of wishing. . . . If I never reach another milestone, and the Giants finally win a World Series—that's all I could ask for. I'd be complete."

Chapter Eight

Making Home Run History

The 2001 season got off to a great start for Barry. He very quietly began to hit home runs on a consistent basis. As he got heated up, so did his bat. Soon the balls were flying out of the parks, and Barry was on fire. On several occasions, he even hit two or three in a single game. It was unlike anything anyone had seen before.

Before long the Giants realized that Barry was approaching a significant milestone in his career—500 home runs. Only sixteen major-league players had ever reached that number. Barry began feeling the pressure each time he stepped up to bat. "You go up there and you feel like you're onstage by yourself," he said. On April 16, during a game in Milwaukee, Wisconsin, Barry hit number 499.

He returned home, and on April 17, in front of 41,059 fans, the largest crowd ever to sit in Pac Bell Park, Barry Bonds made history. In the eighth inning, Barry went deep off of Dodgers pitcher Terry Adams to join the prestigious 500 home run club. This club has just nineteen members, including legends Hank Aaron, Reggie Jackson, Harmon Killebrew, Mickey Mantle, Mark McGwire, Babe Ruth, and Ted Williams.

Barry got home run number 500 with a splash—literally. The two-run drive flew right into McCovey Cove, just beyond the right-field fence and into San Francisco Bay. Dozens of fans on boats, personal watercraft, and even surfboards scurried for the ball as it plunked into the water.

"Deep to right field," yelled announcer Jon Miller. "This is on its way to McCovey Cove, number five hundred!" The crowd, which had been waiting for weeks in anticipation of the big event, erupted as the Giants took a 3–2 lead. Barry rounded the bases and proudly jumped with both feet on home plate. From there he hugged teammate Rich Aurilia, who had scored just ahead of him. Then he embraced his mom, dad, and Bobby Jr. Next the left-field fence opened up, and a golf cart carrying Willie Mays and Willie McCovey—also members of the "500 Club"— pulled up and joined the festivities at home plate. The crowd, waving orange rally towels that had been passed out before the game, went crazy as they chanted, "Barry! Barry! Barry!"

The two Willies were overjoyed to share in the celebration. "When I touched him, he was still shaking. That shows me he realizes what history is all about," said Willie Mays.

Afterward Barry described what had happened. "[Terry Adams] threw me a slider in. I couldn't believe I hit it because everything was in slow motion. I was looking up and the ball was in midair and it wasn't going anywhere. Then, when it got to the people, I said, 'Wow.'" Barry said that having number 500 also be the game-winning hit made it all the more special.

---

66 *It was great to hit 500 in McCovey Cove. I really wanted to jump over the railing, give Mac [Willie McCovey] a hug, and say, 'I did it in your house.' The other thing is, I got to do it in Willie Mays's yard.* 99

—BARRY BONDS

Barry's home run streak continued. Just a month later, on May 21, Barry tied a major-league record when he hit his eighth home run in just five games. At one point within that stretch, he even hit homers in five of six at bats.

On May 30, at a packed Pac Bell Park, Barry faced Arizona Diamondbacks pitcher Robert Ellis. Barry led off the second inning with the Giants down 2–0. Barry stepped up and pounded the first pitch straight into McCovey Cove. When he touched home plate, he looked over to Willie McCovey, who was sitting in the front row near the San Francisco dugout. McCovey stood up, waved back at Barry, and joined the other fans in giving Barry a well-deserved standing ovation. Bonds wasn't done yet, and he homered a second time later in the game. This one went deep into the center-field seats. It was Barry's twenty-eighth home run of the year. This time when Barry got through rounding the bases, he ran over to McCovey's seat to shake his hand. The crowd went wild as two Giants legends took a moment to acknowledge each other.

After hitting a major-league-record seventeen home runs in the month of May, Barry was named player of the month for the eighth time in his career. By this time, fans started to realize that if Barry kept up his pace, he might just be able to break Mark McGwire's single-season home run record.

Even McGwire was impressed. "What he's done, it's absolutely phenomenal," he said of Bonds's incredible home run pace. "It's in the stratosphere. It's almost like he's playing T-ball." Barry's dream season just kept on getting better and better as he entered the All-Star break with a major-league-record thirty-nine home runs. For his efforts, he was the National League's leading vote getter for his tenth All-Star game.

Despite the mounting pressure, Barry maintained his incredible pace through August and into September. Then on September 11, 2001, tragedy struck America when terrorists hijacked four airliners and attacked the World Trade Center in

New York and the Pentagon in Washington, D.C. Baseball took a backseat to the sad events that unfolded and all play was suspended for a week.

DURING THE 2001 SEASON, BARRY

- hit more home runs (seventeen) on Thursday than any other day;
- became the oldest player to lead either league in home runs;
- became the oldest player to hit fifty, sixty, and seventy home runs;
- became the fastest player in a season to reach the thirty-, forty-, fifty-, sixty-, and seventy-homer plateaus.

When baseball resumed, Barry picked up where he had left off. He was on the verge of breaking Mark McGwire's single-season home run record of seventy, and the fans started to get anxious. Everywhere Barry went, the fans lined up to see him make history. "I've never been through anything like this," said Barry in an interview. "If I knew what I was doing, I would have done it a long time ago."

On October 3, 2001, the Houston Astros walked Barry three times. With 172 walks, Barry surpassed Babe Ruth's single-season walk record of 170. While the record was significant, it also represented a problem for Barry—pitchers simply did not want to pitch to him.

As Barry neared McGwire's record, opposing teams began to walk him more and more often. It got to the point that when his daughters came to his games, they held up signs that read: "Please pitch to our daddy."

Barry finally got number seventy on October 4 at Houston, off of pitcher Wilfredo Rodriguez. Numbers seventy-one and seventy-two then came the very next night at home against Dodgers pitcher Chan Ho Park. When Barry hit home runs seventy-one and seventy-two, two records were set that night. The first was Barry's, and the second was the fact that the game itself wound up becoming the longest nine-inning game in major-league history. Partly because of the prolonged cheering for Barry's record, the game had lasted four hours and twenty-seven minutes.

It didn't take long for the outpouring of celebratory congratulations to come streaming in from players, friends, family, and even politicians who wanted to wish Barry well. One of the most significant comments, however, came from the man who Barry had just surpassed in the record books. "He's totally blown away what I did," said McGwire.

"I just felt grateful to share something with someone I have a lot of respect for," said Barry of McGwire. "I felt proud to be on the same level with Mark. I just felt proud. I don't know how else to explain it."

On the downside, Barry's new record cost him a cool $100,000. Back in May, Barry jokingly bet teammate Shawon Dunston a brand-new Mercedes-Benz that he would not be able to break the record. Shawon thought otherwise. "The whole team was stretching, and [Barry] just looked at me like I'm crazy, like he always does," Dunston said. "I said, 'If you do break the record you can buy me a new Mercedes-Benz.'" Barry, who later made good on the bet and bought his friend the new luxury car, said he was happy he lost.

With the record broken and the pressure off, Barry could finally relax. By now it wasn't the media that was all over him, though, it was the fans. His contract with the Giants was up at the end of 2001. The fans did not want him to leave San Francisco, and they were determined to let him know how much they cared. During the final few weeks of the season, the fans had been serenading owner Peter Magowan with chants of, "Sign him!" and, "Four more years!" Barry remained diplomatic. After hitting his record-breaking home run, he said, "It's an honor to play with a bunch of guys like this behind me. I'll play for you anytime, any day of the week, any hour, any year." The only question was whether the team would be able to afford another hefty contract.

❝ *We have never seen a season like this in our lifetime and we probably never will again.* ❞
—NED COLLETTI, GIANTS ASSISTANT GENERAL MANAGER

As far as the regular season was concerned, the Giants had a solid record of 90–72. It wasn't quite enough, though, and they finished out of the postseason yet again. Barry finished the season with seventy-three homers and, perhaps even more impressively, he topped Babe Ruth's eighty-one-year-old record for slugging percentage with an astounding .863. The record was very meaningful to Barry, and it signified his amazing ability as a batter. Whether he was drawing walks, hitting singles, or slamming home runs, Barry found a way to get on base. In addition, he wound up with a career high 137 RBIs and an impressive .328 average. He also had 177 walks and an on-base percentage of .515—the best in the majors since 1957. He even became the first player ever to hit homers in five straight games twice in one season. For his accomplishments, it was no surprise that Barry won a record fourth MVP award. With the country still mourning the aftermath of the September 11 terrorist attacks, Barry appropriately said, "This MVP just to me symbolizes the strength of a nation."

Dusty Baker summed up Barry's accomplishments: "It's like in hockey in an overtime game, you anticipate [Wayne] Gretzky will score. In basketball, you know Michael Jordan is going to take the shot. In football, you know Jerry Rice is going to catch the pass. That's the real superstar—when everyone knows he's going to get the ball and he still scores or makes the play."

Chapter Nine

Number 600 and the World Series

That off-season, Barry tested the free agent market. Several teams inquired about his services, but in the end he re-signed with the Giants for a whopping five-year, $90 million contract extension. "My heart has always been here," said Barry. "No amount of money would make me leave San Francisco, to be honest with you. I always wanted to stay a San Francisco Giant. Unless there was a blockbuster, out-of-the-world offer, I wasn't going to leave. All I want now is a World Series ring."

Barry came into the 2002 season cool and collected. He picked up right where he had left off the season before by hitting a pair of homers in each of his first two games of the year—making him the first player ever to hit two homers in back-to-back games at the start of a season. Fans began the countdown to number seventy-four.

CHASING HANK

Barry starred in a national television commercial that aired during the 2002 Super Bowl. In it, Barry is alone at night in Pac Bell Park, taking batting practice. He suddenly hears a mysterious whispering voice warning him that he shouldn't pursue the all-time career home run record held by Hank Aaron. Bonds then turns and looks up to the announcer's booth, and it's revealed that the voice belongs to none other than Hank Aaron. The funny spot helped to soften Barry's image.

On June 5, Barry blasted his 587th home run in the top of the third inning against the San Diego Padres. With that one, he passed legendary Orioles slugger Frank Robinson to move into fourth place on the all-time home run list. Next on the list was Willie Mays, with 660.

Just two months later, on August 9, in front of his home crowd, Barry again made history. This time he hit one deep off of Pirates right-hander Kip Wells in the sixth inning to notch his 600th career home run. After hitting it, he simply stood and admired its beauty as it sailed 421 feet into the center-field seats. The fans scrambled for the ball, and when one man finally grabbed the ball in triumph, he emerged with cuts on his face, legs, arms, and hand.

Barry had become just one of four men in the history of baseball ever to reach the 600-home-run plateau, joining Willie Mays, Babe Ruth, and Hank Aaron. He was 155 home runs away from surpassing Aaron's all-time record of 755. "To be in that select group is great, but nothing's more satisfying than doing it in front of 40,000 friends here in San Francisco," said Bonds after the game. "I don't think that it could ever be more gratifying than that."

"I tell [Barry] home runs are there to be hit. If you pass me, pass Ruth, pass Hank, then just go ahead and do it. . . . This is just baseball."

—Willie Mays

While the season was going along well for Barry, he got some devastating news in his personal life. His father, Bobby, had been diagnosed with lung cancer. Barry knew that his dad was strong, but he still worried about his father's health. He tried to stay focused on baseball.

Led by Barry's and Jeff Kent's bats and an outstanding pitching staff, the Giants finally got back into the postseason in 2002. After holding off the Dodgers in the opening round wild-card game, the Giants faced the Atlanta Braves in the National

League Division Series. The Giants took game one but then lost the next two before rallying to win the last pair and take the series. It was the first time Barry had ever tasted postseason success, and it tasted pretty good.

It was on to the National League Championship Series. The Giants were up against the St. Louis Cardinals. Nearly every time the Cardinals intentionally walked Bonds, Benito Santiago, who followed him in the batting order, came through with a solid hit. The Giants won in five games. With that, the Giants were in the World Series. They would face off against the Anaheim Angels, who were making their first-ever World Series appearance.

How has Barry Bonds been able to produce so much power at the plate? In recent years, he has put a lot more arc in his swing, and he always aims to hit a pitch deep into the field. In addition, he follows a strict diet of healthy food to give him energy. He also benefits from shorter fences that have been built at many new ballparks. Finally, Barry stands closer to home plate than many other batters. This stance helps him to pull pitches on the outside half of the plate with power.

The all-California matchup kicked off with Barry showing critics that he wouldn't crumble under the pressure of his first World Series. He pounded a home run on his first swing in game one. The Giants took the game 4–3, only to see the Angels rally to take games two and three. San Francisco responded with a win in game four and then took game five as well, thanks to a pair of homers from Jeff Kent. The Giants were just one win away from winning their first World Series.

In game six, the Giants roared to a 5–0 lead by the seventh inning. Barry hit his fourth homer of the series, and the Giants were poised to win it all. That's when things started to go wrong. The Angels fought back behind their famous "Rally Monkey." (The Rally Monkey was a humorous film clip of a dancing monkey shown on the scoreboard to inspire the Angels to come from behind and win.) They got three runs in the seventh and three more in the eighth to earn a shocking 6–5 victory. The stunned Giants could only look on in disbelief as they watched what turned out to be the greatest comeback by a team facing elimination in World Series history.

With the series tied at three games apiece, the Giants still had a shot to win it all in game seven. Barry tried to rally his troops, but the Angels had too much momentum. Their pitching was solid, and they took the game 4–1 to win the series. Barry was devastated, but at least no one could say he was the reason for his team's loss. He batted .356 in the postseason, with a record eight home runs, sixteen RBIs, and a record twenty-seven walks.

In the locker room after the game, reporters asked him what he thought about his first World Series. "I'm not going to lie. It was fun," said Bonds. "I had a good time. I'd like to come back again." When they asked how he felt about his performance and the team's loss, he said, "You can't be mad for doing your best. Disappointed, maybe, but not mad. . . . So I tip my hat to [the Angels]. They played well."

The Angels were founded in Los Angeles in 1961, and from 1965 to 1996 they were known as the California Angels. They moved to Anaheim and changed their name in 1997. The organization has won four division crowns—in 1979, 1982, 1986, and 2002—and its first World Series title in 2002.

With the season finished, Barry's final stats were tallied. Although he hadn't broken the home run record again, Barry had still posted huge numbers during the regular season. He finished the year with forty-six home runs and 110 RBIs. He also captured his first career batting title (awarded to the player with the league's highest batting average) with an amazing .370 average. In addition, he even set a major-league record for reaching base an amazing 58.3 percent of the time—shattering the previous mark of 55.3 percent held by Hall of Famer Ted Williams. In the end, Barry became baseball's first five-time MVP, winning the award unanimously.

Barry was thrilled. "Oh, wow," he said, "I'm trying to figure out why a thirty-eight-year-old player is still playing like this. I'm overjoyed. I'm . . . very pleased, especially after coming off a seventy-three-home-run year and being able to stay consistent. It's very gratifying."

Chapter | Ten

"Barry's Barry . . . "

After the World Series, the typical questions arose as to why Barry's team just couldn't win the big one. Other questions followed, including some about Barry's attitude toward his teammates. Reporters even asked about the special $3,000 leather massage chair Barry has in the Giants locker room. He often sits in it for several hours before games, icing his neck and watching his big-screen TV on the floor. All other members of the team, meanwhile, sit on folding metal chairs.

"It's just a massage chair," Bonds had said previously. "[Ken Griffey Jr.] had one in Seattle and nobody said anything. I have one and it's in the papers. But you know what? My teammates don't care. My manager doesn't care. . . . I have bulging discs in my back. I'd be all locked up if I sat in those metal chairs all day. I might as well make sure my back is OK so I can perform at my best."

In addition to having the special chair, Barry also works with his own trainer before games instead of stretching with the rest of the team. He eats food prepared by a nutritionist rather than eating the team meal provided in the clubhouse. And he often rides the bus with the team's broadcasters, trainers, and coaches instead of riding on the players' bus.

Barry can be moody. At times, reporters have found him to be friendly and generous. At other times, he can be quick-tempered and impatient. He treats his sport as a job and is so focused on his work that he doesn't always greet his teammates in the clubhouse. While his attitude might upset some players, Barry believes that as a superstar, he has earned the right to be aloof. In a *Sports Illustrated* interview, Jeff Kent echoed what Dusty Baker and others often said: "Barry's Barry." In other words, he is what he is and you just have to accept him.

Barry doesn't seem upset by the fact that other players may not like his behavior. He said, "I like to be against the odds. I'm not afraid to be lonely at the top. With me, it's just the satisfaction of the game. Just performance."

Following the World Series and the swarm of media attention, Barry left San Francisco to play in Japan. He took part in an exhibition series between major-league All-Stars and their Japanese counterparts. During a home run competition, Barry showed his friendlier side. He faced Japanese batting star Hideki

Matsui in the contest. In the first of two rounds, Barry managed to hit four homers, while Matsui hit only one. In a break before the second round, Barry approached Matsui and gave him a shoulder rub and a little advice. In the second round, Matsui improved and got four homers. Barry matched him with another four of his own. Afterward Matsui said, "I really admire [Barry's] power, and he sure is the number one hitter in the world. He told me to relax and also told me to close my shoulder. It was a memorable day for me."

Barry returned from Japan to find some major changes taking place within the Giants. First, team manager Dusty Baker signed on to manage the Chicago Cubs. Then Jeff Kent signed as a free agent with the Houston Astros. Kent, who hit thirty-seven homers in 2002, had played an important role in the team's lineup. Often batting just behind Barry, he had forced more opposing pitchers to pitch to Barry rather than walk him.

In November 2002, Felipe Alou was named as the new Giants manager. Alou had played with the Giants in the early 1960s alongside Willie Mays. Some wondered how Barry would adjust to having a new manager for only the third time in his major-league career. But Alou didn't seem concerned. "I don't see Barry Bonds having any problem as long as he continues to produce and be excellent and maybe the best player in the game," he said. "I don't see why anybody would have any problem with a man like that."

Barry kicked off the 2003 season with a renewed sense of urgency. He enjoyed playing for Alou and liked the look of his team as they entered the season. Barry wanted more than ever to win a World Series this year and was determined to do everything in his power to achieve that goal.

❝ *I don't know how [Barry] can live with not being pitched to. Sometimes he goes days without seeing a strike and when he does see it, it's usually in the corner, down. I only know right now he's gaining on everybody. I hope I'll be alive and able to say he was the greatest player ever.* **❞**

—FELIPE ALOU

On June 23, Barry stole his 500th base in a game against the Dodgers. After the historic steal, Barry uprooted the base from the ground and waved it to the crowd. Barry won a showdown with Dodgers closing pitcher Eric Gagne that night, also scoring the winning run on Benito Santiago's single in the eleventh inning to give his team a 3–2 victory. "Gagne's one of the best closers you'll ever see," Bonds said afterward. "I thought about [stealing second] because you never know if you're going to get another chance against him. When I got to second base, my only thought was that we had a chance to win."

Barry became the thirty-sixth player to steal 500 bases, but the historic steal put him into a much more exclusive club. In baseball history, no other player had ever reached the "500-500 club" (500 home runs and 500 steals). In fact, Barry also remains the only member of the "400-400 club." The accomplishment was just another sign of Barry's monster talents. To make the evening even more special, Bobby, who continued his struggle with health problems, made a surprise appearance in the Giants' clubhouse to cheer on his son.

SOLD!

On June 25, 2003, Barry's seventy-third home run ball went up for sale. When the historic home run ball had fallen into the outfield seats in October 2001, it first landed in Alex Popov's glove. The ball was ripped out of his glove, however, and after a struggle, it wound up in the hands of Patrick Hayashi. Afterward Popov and Hayashi both claimed the ball as their own, and they went to court to sort things out. A judge ruled that the two men had to sell the ball in an auction and split the proceeds. In the end the ball was sold to Todd McFarlane for $517,500. McFarlane was also the proud owner of Mark McGwire's seventieth and Sammy Sosa's sixty-sixth home run balls. He said that he planned to call the Baseball Hall of Fame so that he could loan them the ball to display for visitors.

After the game, Alou observed, "In that last at bat, [Barry] was dominant without hitting a home run. I hope people don't judge Barry only by the home runs he hits. He's a supreme player."

In late July, personal concerns overshadowed Barry's play. Bobby's chemotherapy was making him feel weak and sick. He'd had an operation to remove a brain tumor in April and now had to have open-heart surgery for a problem unrelated to the cancer. Barry was beside himself with worry. Bobby's illness was so severe that he was no longer able to watch over Barry's playing. Barry had grown very used to his father's presence as a coach with the Giants. "I've never played baseball without my dad," said Barry. "Now I play alone. I could take a bad swing on the field, and my dad could make a phone call in five seconds and tell me what's wrong. There's no more phone calls."

Barry knew his dad was a fighter and vowed to be with him every step of the way. At one point, Barry left the team for five days to be with his father. Unfortunately, the team suffered without him and lost every game they played that week. One reporter noted that as of August 21, Bonds's thirty-eight home runs made up more than 25 percent of the team's total homers for the season.

On August 23, 2003, Bobby died. He was just fifty-seven years old. The baseball world was shocked and saddened by his death, and the news of his passing was featured on newspapers and television broadcasts throughout the nation. The Giants and fans observed a moment of silence on the field the evening of the twenty-third. Baseball commissioner Bud Selig said, "All of baseball mourns the passing of Bobby Bonds. He was a great player, who with speed and power helped redefine the game. He was a credit to baseball. We will miss him."

When Barry returned to Pac Bell Park on September 2, the fans gave him a standing ovation as he was introduced. He turned in a good performance, hitting a double and then scoring the first run of the game later in the inning. Afterward Alou said, "Barry is a man on a mission. He has been for a long time. But with him and his father, baseball was everything. I think the game will mean even more to him now."

When Bobby and Barry's statistics are compared to those of other father-son baseball pairs, the results are very impressive. Barry and his dad are the all-time leaders in home runs, RBIs, and stolen bases.

On September 15, Barry hit his 655th career home run, putting him just 100 behind Hank Aaron's record. He was also just five homers away from Willie Mays's 660. In the bottom of the sixth inning of that game, Bonds also had his 2,063rd walk to become number two on the all-time list of career walks behind Rickey Henderson. Barry's feats gave the team enough momentum to come back from behind and beat the San Diego Padres 8–7.

"He might be the most complete baseball player we've ever seen," said Ned Colletti, the team's vice president and assistant general manager, of Bonds. "One day, we'll all be telling our grandchildren how fortunate we were to watch Barry Bonds play baseball."

500-500 CLUB

With 500 home runs and 500 stolen bases, Barry is in a class all by himself. No other player has reached 500-500. A player would have to average thirty-three homers and thirty-three stolen bases per year for fifteen years to match his 500-500 record! In fact, there are just three other players in history to reach even the 300-300 club:

Player	HRs	SBs
Willie Mays	660	338
Bobby Bonds	332	461
Andre Dawson	438	314

The Giants wound up finishing the season with an impressive 100–61 overall record, good enough for first place in the National League West Division. They finished eight and a half games ahead of the second-place Arizona Diamondbacks.

With that, the team then took on the Florida Marlins in the National League Divisional Series. The Giants were heavily favored to win the best-of-five series. As part of the Marlins' defensive strategy, they walked Barry again and again, preventing him from getting many chances to drive in runs. The Giants started off well, winning game one 2–0. They seemed to lose momentum, though, and lost game two 9–5 and game three 4–3. In the fourth game, the teams seemed evenly matched, and the score was tied at 5–5 at the end of the seventh inning. But by the end of the eighth, the Marlins had a 7–5 lead. The Giants began the ninth with a run, and after two outs, J. T. Snow was at second base and Jeffrey Hammonds was at bat. Hammonds hit a single to left field and Snow headed for home. The Marlins left fielder grabbed the ball and heaved it to catcher Ivan Rodriguez. Snow flung himself at home plate, but Rodriguez hung on to the ball and made the tag to put an end to the game and the Giants' World Series hopes. Barry could only watch the scene unfold from the dugout. He finished the series with just two hits in nine at bats, along with a frustrating eight walks.

Barry, who had a season filled with unbelievable highs as well as unbelievable lows, finished the 2003 season by hitting .341 with forty-five home runs and ninety RBIs. He led the league with his .749 slugging percentage, .529 on-base percentage, and 148 walks. Following the disappointing ending to the season, he went home to relax and spend time with his family. Then in November, he was shocked to win his sixth MVP award, putting him truly in a league of his own. Rumors began to circulate that Barry was ready to retire. But with 658 career homers and just under 100 more needed to surpass Hank Aaron as baseball's all-time home run champ, Barry has said he will be back to make history. He's tough, he's determined, and he's a winner.

The Greatest Ever?

Barry Bonds is simply the best. When he is compared to Babe Ruth, Ted Williams, Joe DiMaggio, and even Willie Mays, he stands above all others. While many of those players were dominant in one area, such as hitting, Barry dominates every aspect of his sport. Not only can he hit for power, he can hit for average, steal bases, play Gold Glove–caliber left field, and get on base to score runs. Simply put, Barry can do it all. He might just be the most well-rounded player in history. In fact, he is one of only four male athletes in the four major professional sports of baseball, basketball, football, and hockey to win six MVP awards, joining the National Basketball Association's Kareem Abdul-Jabbar (6), as well as the National Hockey League's Wayne Gretzky (9) and Gordie Howe (6).

The player of the decade for the 1990s, Barry has continued to dominate his sport in the new millennium and shows no sign of slowing down. He works out and trains relentlessly. His bat speed is still lightning quick and his arm still resembles a cannon in left field. In fact, as the years have gone by, many experts have felt that Barry has only gotten better.

In spite of all his success, Barry Bonds is still haunted by his inability to win a World Series ring. It seems that his only remaining goals in baseball are to win a ring and break Hank Aaron's all-time home run record of 755. On May 28, 2006, Barry hit his 715th home run to pass Babe Ruth's career total of 714, moving him into second place behind Aaron. Overall, Barry Bonds is a sure-thing Hall of Famer whose power and speed have made him the greatest baseball player of the modern era.

Barry is a "Giant" in the community as well as on the field. He gives much of his time and money to help those in need. Among his many charitable interests are the United Way of the Bay Area, with which he has formed the Bonds Family Foundation (BFF). The BFF's goal is to encourage, promote, and fund programs designed to improve educational achievements, standard of living, and quality of life for African American youth within the San Francisco Bay Area. The program's emphasis is technology-based solutions.

Barry also enjoys buying fifty bleacher seats per game in a section of Pac Bell Park out in left field called "The Bonds Squad," where kids in his foundation can enjoy watching Giants games. When Barry takes the field in the first inning, he often looks up and tips his cap to the kids in his special section. This program has made him a hero to many kids for reasons above and beyond the game of baseball.

All in all, Barry Bonds is a superstar and is among the very best of the best. And who knows? Maybe Barry's son, Nikolai, will one day follow in his father's footsteps the same way that Barry did with Bobby. If all goes well, we should be hearing about Nikolai trying to break his father's home run record in the year 2030. Stay tuned!

PERSONAL STATISTICS

Name:

Barry Lamar Bonds

Born:

July 24, 1964

Height:

6' 2"

Weight:

228 lbs.

Bats:

Left

Throws:

Left

Awards:

All-Star games (12): 1990, 1992–1998, 2000–2003
MVP awards (6): 1990, 1992, 1993, 2001, 2002, 2003
Gold Glove awards (8): 1990, 1991, 1992, 1993, 1994, 1996, 1997, 1998

BATTING STATISTICS

Year	Team	Avg	G	AB	Runs	Hits	2B	3B	HR	RBI	SB
1986	Pitt	.223	113	413	72	92	26	3	16	48	36
1987	Pitt	.261	150	551	99	144	34	9	25	59	32
1988	Pitt	.283	144	538	97	152	30	5	24	58	17
1989	Pitt	.248	159	580	96	144	34	6	19	58	32
1990	Pitt	.301	151	519	104	156	32	3	33	114	52
1991	Pitt	.292	153	510	95	149	28	5	25	116	43
1992	Pitt	.311	140	473	109	147	36	5	34	103	39
1993	SF	.336	159	539	129	181	38	4	46	123	29
1994	SF	.312	112	391	89	122	18	1	37	81	29
1995	SF	.294	144	506	109	149	30	7	33	104	31
1996	SF	.308	158	517	122	159	27	3	42	129	40
1997	SF	.291	159	532	123	155	26	5	40	101	37
1998	SF	.303	156	552	120	167	44	7	37	122	28
1999	SF	.262	102	355	91	93	20	2	34	83	15
2000	SF	.306	143	480	129	147	28	4	49	106	11
2001	SF	.328	153	476	129	156	32	2	73	137	13
2002	SF	.370	143	403	117	149	31	2	46	110	9
2003	SF	.341	130	390	111	133	22	1	45	90	7
	Totals	.297	2,569	8,725	1,941	2,595	536	74	658	1,742	500

Key: **Avg:** batting average; **G:** games; **AB:** at bats; **2B:** doubles; **3B:** triples; **HR:** home runs; **RBI:** runs batted in; **SB:** stolen bases

BARRY BONDS'S HOME RUNS
DURING THE 2001 SEASON

No.	Date	Opponent	Pitcher
1	April 2	San Diego	Woody Williams
2	April 12	@San Diego	Adam Eaton
3	April 13	@Milwaukee	Jamey Wright
4	April 14	@Milwaukee	Jimmy Haynes
5	April 15	@Milwaukee	Dave Weathers
6	April 17	Los Angeles	Terry Adams
7	April 18	Los Angeles	Chan Ho Park
8	April 20	Milwaukee	Jimmy Haynes
9	April 24	Cincinnati	Jim Brower
10	April 26	Cincinnati	Scott Sullivan
11	April 29	Chicago	Manny Aybar
12	May 2	@Pittsburgh	Todd Richie
13	May 3	@Pittsburgh	Jimmy Anderson
14	May 4	@Philadelphia	Bruce Chen
15	May 11	New York	Steve Trachsel
16	May 17	@Florida	Chuck Smith
17	May 18	@Atlanta	Mike Remlinger
18	May 19	@Atlanta	Odalis Perez
19	May 19	@Atlanta	Jose Cabrera
20	May 19	@Atlanta	Jason Marquis
21	May 20	@Atlanta	John Burkett
22	May 20	@Atlanta	Mike Remlinger
23	May 21	@Arizona	Curt Schilling
24	May 22	@Arizona	Russ Springer
25	May 24	Colorado	John Thomson
26	May 27	Colorado	Denny Neagle
27	May 30	Arizona	Robert Ellis
28	May 30	Arizona	Robert Ellis
29	June 1	@Colorado	Shawn Chacon
30	June 4	San Diego	Bobby J Jones
31	June 5	San Diego	Wascar Serrano
32	June 7	San Diego	Brian Lawrence
33	June 12	Anaheim	Pat Rapp
34	June 14	Anaheim	Lou Pote
35	June 15	Oakland	Mark Mulder
36	June 15	Oakland	Mark Mulder

37	June 19	@San Diego	Adam Eaton
38	June 20	@San Diego	Rodney Myers
39	June 23	@St. Louis	Daryl Kile
40	July 12	@Seattle	Paul Abbott
41	July 18	Colorado	Mike Hampton
42	July 18	Colorado	Mike Hampton
43	July 26	@Arizona	Curt Schilling
44	July 26	@Arizona	Curt Schilling
45	July 27	@Arizona	Brian Anderson
46	August 1	Pittsburgh	Joe Beimel
47	August 4	Philadelphia	Nelson Figueroa
48	August 7	@Cincinnati	Danny Graves
49	August 9	@Cincinnati	Scott Winchester
50	August 11	@Chicago	Joe Borowski
51	August 14	Florida	Ricky Bones
52	August 16	Florida	AJ Burnett
53	August 16	Florida	Vic Darensbourg
54	August 18	Atlanta	Jason Marquis
55	August 23	@Montreal	Graeme Lloyd
56	August 27	@New York	Kevin Appier
57	August 31	Colorado	John Thomson
58	September 3	Colorado	Jason Jennings
59	September 4	Arizona	Miguel Batista
60	September 6	Arizona	Albie Lopez
61	September 9	@Colorado	Scott Elarton
62	September 9	@Colorado	Scott Elarton
63	September 9	@Colorado	Todd Belitz
64	September 20	Houston	Wade Miller
65	September 23	@San Diego	Jason Middlebrook
66	September 23	@San Diego	Jason Middlebrook
67	September 24	@Los Angeles	James Baldwin
68	September 28	San Diego	Jason Middlebrook
69	September 29	San Diego	Chuck McElroy
70	October 4	@Houston	Wilfredo Rodriguez
71	October 5	Los Angeles	Chan Ho Park
72	October 5	Los Angeles	Chan Ho Park
73	October 7	Los Angeles	Dennis Springer

FIELDING STATISTICS

Year	Team	Pos	G	C	PO	A	E	DP	FLD%
1986	Pitt	OF	110	294	280	9	5	2	.983
1987	Pitt	OF	145	350	330	15	5	3	.986
1988	Pitt	OF	136	303	292	5	6	0	.980
1989	Pitt	OF	156	385	365	14	6	1	.984
1990	Pitt	OF	150	358	338	14	6	2	.983
1991	Pitt	OF	150	337	321	13	3	1	.991
1992	Pitt	OF	139	317	310	4	3	0	.991
1993	SF	OF	157	322	310	7	5	0	.984
1994	SF	OF	112	211	198	10	3	2	.986
1995	SF	OF	143	297	279	12	6	2	.980
1996	SF	OF	152	302	286	10	6	1	.980
1997	SF	OF	159	305	290	10	5	0	.984
1998	SF	OF	155	308	301	2	5	0	.984
1999	SF	OF	96	186	178	5	3	2	.984
2000	SF	OF	141	265	254	8	3	4	.989
2001	SF	OF	143	260	246	8	6	1	.977
2002	SF	OF	135	253	241	4	8	2	.968
2003	SF	OF	123	243	236	5	2	2	.992
	Total		2,502	5,296	5,055	155	86	25	.984

Key: Pos: position; G: games; C: chances (balls hit to a position); PO: putouts; A: assists; E: errors; DP: double plays; FLD%: fielding percentage

BIBLIOGRAPHY

Associated Press. "Stop, thief!" *CNNSI.com*. June 24, 2003.
    <http://sportsillustrated.cnn.com/baseball/news/2003
    /06/23/dodgers_giants_ap/> (December 1, 2003).

"Bobby's Cancer Taking Mental Toll on Barry." *ESPN.com*.
    June 11, 2003. <http://espn.go.com/nlb/news/2003
    /0611/1566431.html> (December 1, 2003).

Gloster, Rob. "Bonds Extends Record with No. 73." *South Coast
    Today*. October 8, 2001. <http://www.s-t.com/daily
    /10-01/10-08-01/c13sp115.htm> (September 22, 2003).

Hersch, Hank. "30/30 Vision." *CNNSI.com*. June 25, 1990.
    <http://sportsillustrated.cnn.com/features/cover
    /flashbacks/bonds_vision/> (December 1, 2003).

Muskat, Carrie. "Cover Report: Barry Bonds." *USAToday.com*.
    April 15, 1997. <http://www.usatoday.com/sports
    /baseball/sbbw5215.htm> (December 1, 2003).

Pearlman, Jeff. "Appreciating Bonds." *CNNSI.com*. June 5, 2000.
    <http://sportsillustrated.cnn.com/features/cover
    /flashbacks/bonds_appreciating> (December 1, 2003).

Pearlman, Jeff. "It's a Wrap!" *Sports Illustrated*. October 15, 2001.
    <http://sportsillustrated.cnn.com/features/2001
    /sportsman/flashbacks/bonds/wrap> (December 1, 2003).

Reilly, Rick. "He Loves Himself Barry Much." *CNNSI.com*.
    August 27, 2001. <http://sportsillustrated.cnn.com
    /inside_game/magazine/life_of_reilly/news/2001/08/21
    /life_of_reilly> (December 1, 2003).

Rovell, Darren. "McFarlane Wins Auction for Historic Bonds Ball."
    ESPN.com. June 25, 2003. <http://sports.espn.go.com
    /espn/print?id=1572871&type=news> (August 29, 2003).

Savage, Jeff. *Barry Bonds*. Minneapolis: Lerner Publications,
    2002.

"Sold! McFarlane Pays $450,000 for Bonds' 73rd HR Ball."
    CNNSI.com. June 25, 2003. <http://sportsillustrated
    .cnn.com/baseball/news/2003/06/25/bonds_73ball
    _ap/> (August 29, 2003).

Travers, Steven. *Barry Bonds: Baseball's Superman*. Champaign,
    IL: Sports Publishing, 2002.

Verducci, Tom. "600 and Counting." *Sports Illustrated*, August
    19, 2002, 42–44.

WEB SITES

Barry Bonds Central

www.bondscentral.com

This fan site for Barry Bonds gives quotes, photos, stats, and much more.

San Francisco Giants: The Official Site

sanfrancisco.giants.mlb.com

The official Web site of the San Francisco Giants has a special section for kids.

Junior Baseball

www.juniorbaseball.com

The Web site of Junior Baseball *magazine includes information about Barry Bonds and other baseball greats, baseball resources, and games to play.*

Baseball Almanac

www.baseball-almanac.com/players/player.php?p=bondsba01

Look here for facts and statistics about Barry Bonds.

INDEX